Bones and Sea Dog

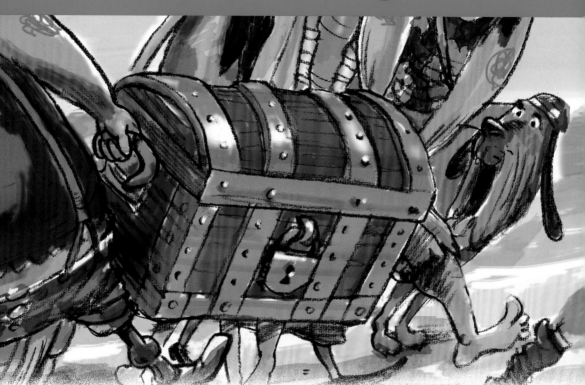

Written by Lisa Thompson
Pictures by Craig Smith and Lew Keilar

Bones always wanted to be a pirate.

As a puppy, Bones dug holes.

He wasn't looking for bones.

He was looking for treasure.

Bones, the dog, tied a scarf on his head.

He drew a black patch over his eye.

It made him look like a pirate.

Bones looked for pirate ships out to sea.

One day, Bones spotted a tiny, black dot.

The dot turned into a ship.

The ship was flying a pirate flag.

Bones watched and waited.

The ragged pirates came ashore.

They were carrying a heavy,
sea chest.

"Wow! Pirate treasure," said Bones.

The Captain looked for a good place
to bury the treasure.

"Here is the spot," said the Captain.
"Hand me the shovel."

"Shovel?" asked a pirate. "You didn't
tell us to bring a shovel."

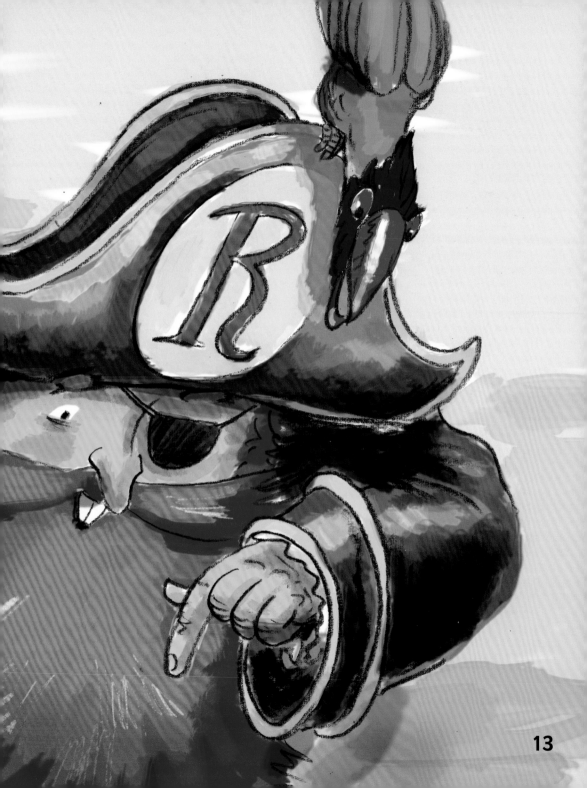

"Split me gizzards!" said the Captain.

"How can we bury the treasure now?"

Bones raced out. In a few seconds, he had dug a deep hole.

"Flying cannonballs!" cried the Captain.

"We have found a new pirate for our crew.
Bones the sea dog!"

The pirates dropped the chest into the hole.

Bones filled up the hole in seconds.

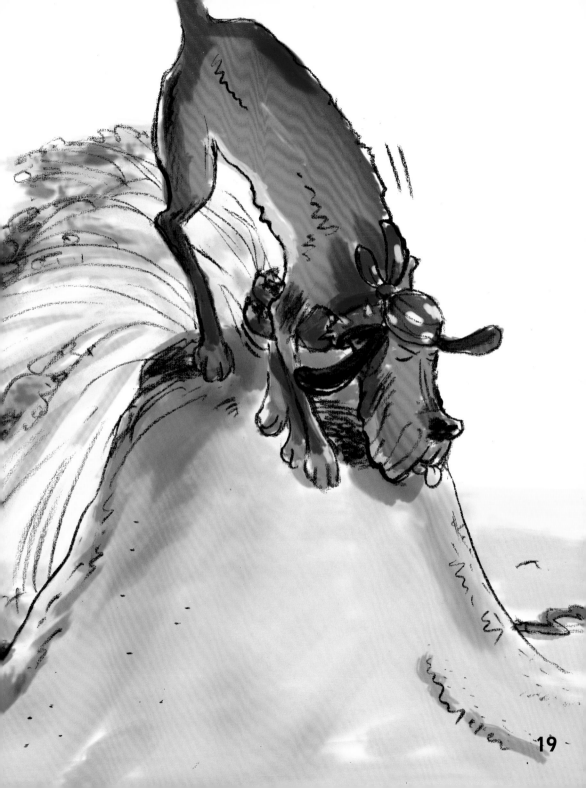

Back on the ship, the Captain found another job for Bones.

Bones kept a lookout for other ships.

He used his eyes and his nose.

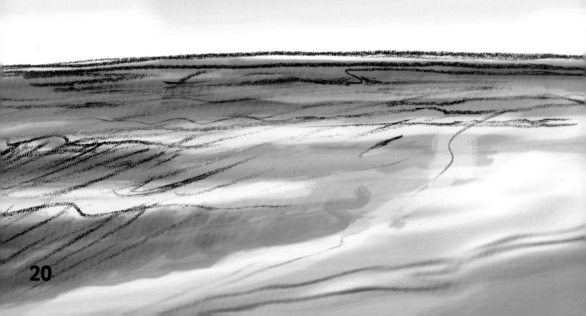

Bones loved his new job.

He could sniff a ship when it was only a dot on the horizon.

But best of all, he still loved digging for treasure.